I0824526

The SDL Review

ANTHOLOGY

2025

SHADOW DOG PRESS

ISBN: 979-8-9935682-1-8

Bulk order discounts are available, at the publisher's discretion, for schools, literacy programs, correctional facilities, mental health and rehabilitation programs, and various other community programs and institutions.

Published in Massachusetts, USA

Shadow Dog Press North Adams, MA 01247
www.ShadowDogPress.com

A SHADOW DOG PRESS PUBLICATION

MASTHEAD

Editor-in-chief — C.B. Mottor

Art Director/Craftsman — J.A. Moda

Admin Extraordinaire — Melanie Bass

CONTENTS

CONTENTS

Happy Here

BY ANGELA TOWNSEND

I am tired of asking what you do for a living. I am morally opposed to assaulting you with cavity searches of your relationship status.

I thought I'd found a balmy palm to stroke small talk on the forehead: "What do you do when you're not here?" But the warm animal escapes under the table.

I want to know what you do that transports you here. I do not mean the party. I do not mean this kitchen, wringing its chicken fingers so we will all be brave as buffalos. I do not mean the wrinkle-proof polyester blouse that you asked three friends to approve. I mean the "here" that bursts like Godzilla through the pet carrier. I mean the "here" that shoots through ceilings. I mean the "here" that fits inside your clutch purse but is too large for the universe. I mean the "here" that you never leave.

I mean to ask you – I am telling you in advance, although we will both still be frightened –

"Do you have something that makes you happy every day?"

I will say "Do you?" for the sake of manners, as though the answer could be "No." We both know better, which is why this is frightening. We know there is not one body laced with capillaries that does not get loose at least once a day.

This is not an appropriate question. I will watch you interrogate the baba ghanoush with a pita chip, digging a labyrinth. I will watch you wish I had asked how you lost that weight, where you bought that cardigan, or if you saw that episode of the zombie show.

If you give me time to ask again, I will answer instead. I will be the naked fool. I will be so afraid, I will drop four fingers in the dip. I will not even realize I am unrolling the crescent roll and letting all the mushrooms out.

"I want you to have things that make you happy every day." I will understate the case, so I don't overwhelm the hosts.

I will tell you I have four crocheted rainbow cats the size of sweet potatoes. I bought one and placed it in the pantry as the centurion of my paper towels. I bought a second and a third. I bought a fourth. I cannot fetch a pouch of shelf-stable cauliflower without seeing these sentinels. They make me happy every day. They make me happy when the linoleum is cold, and my mother is concerned that I may be a Marxist, and there are no valentines in the mailbox. They make me happy when I am the venue for gastrointestinal pageantry, and the test results are unremarkable, and all the syntax has gone on strike.

I will tell you that I have twenty-six letters that are mostly on speaking terms with one another. I trawl them through bayous of self-indulgent dreck. I attempt to debunk my mother's assertions that I have never written anything unworthy of a Pulitzer. I connect them like train cars, knowing they will kidnap me and take me places I did not intend. I give them the passwords to my veins, knowing that they may tie me to the track and go smoke together in the forest. They make me happy when they cooperate and when they moon me. They make me happy when they kiss the sky and when they fling me off the bridge without a bungee. They make me happy when editors reject my hot loaves. They make me happy, because they are not going anywhere, and I get to keep going when I have no idea where this is all going.

I will tell you that I have ancestors who named things, all the way back to the Oldest One who calls stars and wombats by words we are not yet young enough to hear. I will tell you that my insulin pump is named Mavis. My mail carrier is named Butterbean, and someday he will be strong enough to bear this information. My white noise machine is named Ziggy, and every night, a disembodied holy woman named Alexa summons him. My keyboard is named Sweetheart. My best friend is named Ciada Mia, "my breath." My rumpled cat is named Kankipanks. They make me happy because I was made to love in excessive directions. they make me happy because there are friends in the deep and shallow ends.

I will tell you that my mother looks up the number for my local police department if she does not hear from me by 9:15am. I am in my third decade with Type 1 diabetes, which voids my warranty on adulthood. My mother makes me happy because she speaks with equal authority to the Archangel Michael and the unsavory characters making trouble in the CVS parking lot. My mother makes me happy because her eyes do not wander when I take her hiking into my revelations on cottage cheese or sweater socks. She makes me happy because she is evidence that loving a person is an ever-expanding thing, like the universe.

I will tell you that amusing oneself is a human right, although it is under threat from all quarters. I will ask – I am entering the gazebo now, back into the questions – if you have ever noticed how funny the plural of "Pizza Hut" sounds. Say it. Say "Pizza Huts." I will ask if you think it should be "Pizzas Hut."

I will ask if you carry such a torch for some word that you scald your pride, and your boss groans, “you call everything ‘sensational.’” I will ask if you have ever noticed that Subarus and nectarines and adverbs and the vast majority of grandfathers are sensational.

I will not ask who you are dating. I will not ask what you are looking forward to these days. I will ask you to show me the “here” under this place. I will ask the host your birthday so I can send you a rainbow cat.

Angela Townsend works for a cat sanctuary, where she gets to bear witness to mercy for all beings. She is a five-time Pushcart Prize nominee and the 2024 winner of West Trade Review's 704 Prize for Flash Fiction. Her work appears or is forthcoming in Arts & Letters, Blackbird, Epiphany, Peatsmoke Journal, and SmokeLong Quarterly, among others. She graduated from Princeton Seminary and Vassar College and laughs with her poet mother every morning.

belovedmoonchild.wordpress.com

MY FATHER'S CLOSET

—JIM BURNS

The door squeals in resistance
on its metal track
as I slide it open.
The new navy blue suit,
the one he jokingly said
he'd be buried in,
it's not there,
he's being buried in it,
and I'm here searching
for his eyeglasses
because he doesn't look
like himself in the casket
without them.
I've not seen inside this closet
for a long time, if ever,
but Death brings home the prodigal.
There is his tweed jacket.
his everyday work coat,
and there is his cache
of Hawaiian ties, circa 1930s,
garish still, a tattooist's inspiration.
There's a shelf with a box
of family pictures, and another
with papers important to him,
including a message from me

recalling childhood memories
of his return from work,
how I'd waited for him,
ran to the door as he turned the knob,
and buried my face in the blackness
of his heavy winter coat,
its cold exterior cloaking the warmth inside.
The coat was worn, discarded,
but this man, to the world wary of emotion,
had clung to the note,
just as his son's wallet
remained home to his father's response.
Finally, I spot the glasses
with a pile of hospital belongings,
and as I pick them up I notice tear stains,
caused by the heart attack, no doubt,
but he had died with my mother at home sick
and me five hundred miles away at work,
and I stop and wonder
whether that was the source of the tears
as he lie dying alone,
but no time for reflection,
the funeral will be about to begin,
so I grab the spectacles
and when I close the door
it squeals in resistance once more.

THE FENCE

It wasn't exactly overgrown,
the lot on the edge of town,
when after years I returned,
but it's not the unkempt lot
that I speak of,
it's the fence
that stands shakily on it
like a feeble old man
waiting for a bus in a blizzard,
when will it fall?
It was built a half century earlier,
sand moved slowly
through my hourglass of time,
a summer home from college,
nothing much to do,
but for my father
sand was already flowing fast,
already in his fifties and arthritic,
and neither of us
carpenters or painters
or handy with anything
but words and numbers,
or accustomed to working together,
but my father thought it a great idea,
building a fence in our backyard,

so home he came one day
bearing hammers, hails, saws, lumber,
post hole diggers, cement mix to keep
the posts in a permanent
state of tumescence
once we got them into the ground,
and perhaps a magic toad or two
whose back we could rub
and repeat secret oaths
for the good luck we would need,
and so it was that the project was launched,
him working before he went to his job,
over his lunch hour,
after coming home for the day,
and later on until the sun and moon
had made a peaceful transfer of power,
and me when I wanted to work on my tan
or was gently reminded of the task at hand.
And slowly and a bit short of surely
the structure went up—
the ancients erected Stonehenge,
so why couldn't we build a fence—
and it was ready to paint,
a brilliant white
detectable by the earliest satellites
plying deep space.

Funny thing was, it had no purpose,
kept nothing in, let nothing out,
and as it shakily stood in its dotage
was as useful as when it was conceived,
doing nothing but marking the far boundary
of what was once our backyard,
a bleak strip of dirt and grass
punctuated by a metal shed
prone to upending during wind storms,
and salvaged by my father's garden,
but the fence was our summer project,
my father as foreman,
me as his crew,
we did it together,
and when we finished
life seemed better than before.

—JIM BURNS

Jim Burns was born and raised in rural Indiana, received degrees from both Indiana State University and Indiana University, and spent most of his working life as a librarian in Iowa and Florida. After retiring, he turned to a long-held but placed on the back burner interest in writing. Since 2020, has been fortunate enough to have seen about 30 of his pieces, primarily poetry, accepted for publication in print and/or online journals, magazines, blogs, and anthologies. He lives with his wife and dog in Jacksonville, Florida.

THE DECISION AND THE DOG

BY JACKIE FISHMAN

When the nurse on the phone said, "Congratulations, Mrs. Fishman, you are pregnant." I blurted out, "No, I don't want congratulations. I want an abortion."
I was a child myself, even though I was 24. Despite being married to my childhood sweetheart, nothing in my life was settled or secure, and I never believed in the phrase, "It will all work out." There was too much to worry about to let that be my mantra.

I had spent weeks worrying about not getting my period. Pushing tampons into my vagina in the vain hope of finding a spot of blood, a speck of evidence that I might be about to menstruate. Nothing. There were no home pregnancy tests in 1976, so I lived in uncertainty and, yes... fear. Fear of the decision I knew I would make and the resistance I was sure to face. Fear of the judgements from family. And fear of the procedure itself, which had only recently become legal due to the Roe v Wade decision.

Her tone changed instantly; the phone I held turned into a block of ice. She responded with the necessary information to follow up on my request. Still, it did not include the doctor I usually saw. No, her communication was to seek out the local Planned Parenthood office for the procedure I was seeking.

Yes, even though Roe vs. Wade had become the law of the land three years before, this nurse let me know her disapproval by the tone of her voice and her abrupt information. I had a momentary pang of shame. Was I selfish? Did my circumstances trump my desires for my life?

In the back of our two-family home, the funeral home on Main Street churned out the last of its summer funerals, their garbage pails rimming our back fence filled with long-stemmed gladiolus and lilies from the services. Everything felt fertile and alive. And so was I.

Our dog went into heat. Early one evening, we found her copulating with the neighbor's pup, the two of them stuck together at the genitals, facing opposite directions as dogs do when the main event ends. We helped them disengage, and then we looked at each other, laughing. Our Prudence was undoubtedly pregnant as well.

This was not a decision I had any doubts about. I was operating out of fear and disbelief. My husband of three years and I were moving to a new city, Atlanta, for a university administration job he had been offered. We had no health insurance or moving stipend, and his salary was not going to be enough for us to live on. I was still struggling with getting my driver's license. I had decided to quit my teaching career and embark on a career in communications. Reinvention while pregnant seemed impossible.

I visualized myself pregnant and lonely in the apartment we had rented on the car-heavy Buford Highway location where no one ever walked. The decision was clear to me. I had no need to talk about it or even think about it. Much.

Later that night, when we got ready for bed, my husband curled beside me and put his head on my belly.
"Are you sure?" "We can make it work."

These emotional pleas were not changing my mind. I don't know how I got the strength to resist them. It was fear of failure. And a deep-seated ambivalence toward having a child at all. I knew I would be far from all my family and without friends. I could not imagine being pregnant and unemployed in an unfamiliar place where my accent did not match everyone else's. While my husband would be forging his academic career and working long days, I would be alone in our apartment, unemployable and unable to go anywhere… a prisoner of Buford Highway.

Buffalo, N.Y., in the late summer was the only time of the year the landscape was not unforgiving. Heritage Concord grapes burst from the vines on the fence in our backyard. The old and weary trees on the block were leaf-heavy, and the lawns groaned with thick grass, each blade knowing it would not be long before the long sleep of winter.

Between getting our house ready to sell, packing, and having a garage sale, I was able to make the appointment for my abortion. There was no discussion and no more entreaties. I waited my turn in the Planned Parenthood waiting room with a few other young women. One was animated and cracking jokes. She was pretty, blonde, and self-effacing. Her nervousness was lightly coated by her frivolity, and I sensed pain skimming below the surface of her jokes. All these years later, I still remember feeling her sadness through her merriment. I did not respond to her, nor did I laugh. Fear of the unknown is a potent silencing mechanism.

I changed into the requisite paper gown and laid down on the table to be examined. It was determined that I was about ten weeks along. The procedure I had is called vacuum aspiration, and this name describes it clearly. The doctor had bared muscular arms, and I wondered if a great deal of strength would be needed for this procedure. It was painful but brief, about 15 minutes. When it was completed, the doctor left me alone in the room. I felt weak, but I pushed myself to a sitting position and gazed slowly around, startled by the splattered blood that was everywhere announcing victory. There had been a war between my present and my future, and the remains of this battle were all around me. I had emerged victorious.

Soon after, the clinic called my husband to pick me up. Getting into the car slowly, I had nothing to say. I just wanted to lie down and sleep. We arrived home and curled up on our bed. I fell into that dreamless slumber of exhaustion and escape.

Three months later, heavily pregnant Prudence started panting in our modern Buford Highway apartment. It was a Saturday afternoon, and my husband was at the school for a meeting. I hastily arranged a nesting area for our dog and watched over her as she labored and brought forth a sweet, wet puppy. She knew how to clean and nurse the little furry bundle, and then began to pant again. This time was different as the tail and hind legs appeared first and then the rest of the body. She strained and panted, trying to birth the head, and I realized she needed help. Instinctively, I reached around the head still inside her and gently moved it out of her. The pup struggled to its wobbly legs and fell against its mother, exhausted but alive.

Excited, I jumped up and dashed around the apartment, but no one was there to tell. I was elated. I had helped this life come into the world and felt immense joy and accomplishment. I thought about my decision.

With one driver's license, a full-time job with health insurance, and a thirty-year mortgage later, my thoughts about having a baby started to change. The pups had long grown up and settled into permanent homes, and Prudence was spayed. This time, I found myself pregnant and pleased. In late 1979, when the time came to have my daughter, there was no room for doubt. She burst noisily and eagerly into the world. The doctor slid into the room just as she emerged, on his paper bootie-covered feet as if he were in a Marx Brothers movie. He caught her like a fly ball.

A little more than three years after my abortion and Prudence's maternal event, I felt joy and accomplishment when I gave birth to my daughter. I looked at her screwed-up face as I held her warm, wet body and knew I had won the battle for my future again.

The 2022 abortion rally I attended when Roe v. Wade was struck down by the Supreme Court was filled with personal stories about women's abortion journeys, both desperate and heart-wrenching. The speaker asked the crowd to tell their own stories about their abortions. The women I was with encouraged me to speak

up, and I did. However, I protested that my experience had been undramatic and uneventful. Nevertheless, it was my story.

For the first time, I said it aloud: "I had an abortion."

It was a revelation to feel the fellowship of those around me with this utterance. I had not realized the unrecognized shame I had felt. I had come full circle, finally. There was no need to look back in any shame. My body, My choice, My decision, My future. No excuses. And none were ever necessary. Why had I never known this so clearly before?

Indeed, the Supreme Court decision deepened my own acknowledgement of the fact that an unintended pregnancy does not dictate one's future. It always was and always should be My body, My choice.

Jackie Fishman is a retired public affairs executive with a passion for personal essays and creative nonfiction. Her work has been published in Business Insider, Lilith, Jewish Women of Words, and Still Alive!. She is married and lives in Potomac, Maryland. Jackie has two married children, four grandchildren, a cat, and a dog. Her passions are experience-based travel, indie movies, Mah Jong, and pickleball. Some of her more bizarre activities include jumping out of a perfectly good airplane.

THANKS FOR THE EVIDENCE

BY

TESS GODHARDT

Each finger on your calloused hand left an imprint on my neck. I display each red indentation for the officer's flashing camera. Are there any other injuries? I imagine grabbing the butcher's knife from the kitchen drawer nearby, slicing myself from sternum to stomach, peeling my skin open, and pointing his camera to the six years' worth of gouges your sharp words had carved into my insides like tally marks in a prisoner's cell. Blowups of each and every gash would be paraded in front of the jury. You'd get ten years, easy. Your mother would cry, but not because she's raised an abuser. She would weep because her baby boy doesn't deserve to go to jail. Your alcoholic father would remain at home. Ten beers in. Unsurprised by who you've become. The officer patiently waits for the daydream to end. My vocal cords sting as the word "no," makes its way up my sandpapered throat. Yet, the burn is simultaneously soothing. The choking may not get you ten years, but it does get me my freedom.

THE NECKLACE

TESS GODHARDT

The dog died and she bought a necklace.

At first, the necklace would reject any attempt by Mara to bury it beneath her shirt. At first, everyone acknowledged the necklace.

Everyone felt obligated, duty-bound, to make note of the necklace.

They would deliver their standard remarks with an amiable, but satisfied air, and Mara felt obliged to say, "Thank you," as she gritted her teeth, crossed her arms, examined the ground, and pinched the crooks of her elbows.

Then, the necklace would occasionally slip under Mara's clothes.

There, it would nestle into her skin. The onyx pendant falling in line with her sternum, its cool metallic back rhythmically pulsating with her heart. Flashes of silver flickered from Mara's neckline.

Then, Mara feared losing the necklace. In the course of routine, she would unconsciously undo its lobster clasp, unlax her shoulders, and unwind in the weightlessness.

For a brief moment, the necklace was no more.

A reminder of its existence felt like a rapid descent into arctic waters, and yet comforting.

With trembling, but resolute fingers, Mara would re-hook the chain.

Then, few respected the necklace.

“Maybe it’s time to take it off?” the many suggested.

Mara would pull her collar up apologetically and politely change the subject.

They were fortunate to be devoid of any longing to discuss the necklace.

Now, her necklace falls wherever Mara chooses to place it. Though sometimes, unexpectedly, her necklace will sneak out from her blouses.

In those moments, Mara will grasp her pendant with white knuckles, close her eyes, and feel its edges with her thumb.

Now, Mara protects her necklace.

Her necklace is hers to carry.

Now, no one understands her necklace except for her.

Fitz died and Mara forever grieves.

DRYWALL PIECES

TESS GODHARDT

Cecilia sat on the edge of their bed and tried to study the fist-sized hole in the wall. The mush that had replaced her brain made the exercise challenging. Tito's-laceddrips of sweat covered her forehead. She rubbed her temples, half-hoping the act would jumpstart her recollection of the night before and half-hoping the gesture would rid her of the alcohol-induced headache pounding against her fingertips. Neither wish was fulfilled. She resigned to unconsciously rotating her wedding ring like a fidget spinner and eyed the chips of drywall intertwined with the brown, nylon carpet that itched beneath her bare feet.

Well, at least it's not mixed with glass. She smiled at the dark quip. Cecilia's ex-boyfriend had quit smoking cold turkey and navigating his volatile irritability had seemed no different than trying to avoid motion sensor lasers protecting a priceless artifact while blindfolded. For weeks, she armed herself against his erratic outbursts by using his health as the ultimate justification. She shrunk herself down to avoid being detected by his rage. Each dish that clanged into the sink or door shut a bit too forcefully jolted her nerves. After failing to be imperceptible for the umpteenth time, Cecilia was rewarded with a half-empty Rolling Rock careening at her head. She had deftly avoided the bottle, but her athleticism had cost her an hour cleaning up the glass-spiked drywall crumbs. Green slivers pricked the tips of fingers without drawing blood.

When her ex was no longer held hostage by his nicotine addiction, the two would joke about the beer bottle fiasco to friends and family as a testament to the grip cigarettes could have on you. Even after her ex choked her a year later, Cecilia still found the anecdote amusing. Though not in the same way pre-choke Cecilia did. Post-choke Cecilia's humor derived from the unquestioned normalization of an unequivocally callous action. It all seemed so outlandish to her as though she was part of some quirky sitcom.

But Cecilia felt her personal sitcom foray into a dramatic climax as she focused her gaze back on the wall. She swallowed, pushing a knot down her throat and into in her stomach. A photo of her kissing her husband's cheek at a Cubs game on their first date was propped on his nightstand and flooded her peripherals. Her fingers felt the cold, metallic backing of her crescent-shaped necklace. An anniversary gift. Cecilia ran through a list of her husband's gentle traits and behaviors. She continued this exercise while holding her eyes on the wall. Minutes passed on as the fist-shaped hole's edges resisted morphing into a bottleneck.

Eventually, Cecilia broke her gaze and headed to the bedroom closet to grab the handheld vacuum.

Tess Godhardt is an attorney who has always harbored a love for creative writing. When she is not working, she can be found on the basketball court attempting to relive her collegiate glory days or outside throwing the ball for one of her five dogs. One of her short stories can be found in the Bright Flash Literary Review. She lives with her husband in Cedar Creek, Texas.

More from Tess Godhardt

PRETTY POISON

C.B. MOTTOR

I know,
you wanted
a prize-winning
rose in bloom—
not this dandelion
growing from the crack
in your walkway.

Someday you'll learn
pretty petals
laced with pesticides
don't compare to
healing brews
and granted wishes.

DIONYSUS

C.B. MOTTOR

Come,
change my prose
from poison
to purple,
teach me
a new language,
tame my
serpent tongue.
Take this script
I've scratched
in my blood
with this unhallowed bone.
Give me a story
worth sending home.

The name is C.B. Mottor, but you can call her C. She pens raw and evocative poetry and prose driven by lived experience and shaped by chronic illness, mental health struggles, love, loss, and life-altering traumas. She has also been known to dabble in writing dystopian horror novels and screenplays.

Apart from her writing, she shares artistic photography focused on finding beauty in the chaos, celebrating the skin we're in, and exploring what it means to be a perfectly imperfect, deeply flawed, yet hopeful human being.

C is proud to be the founder and EIC of Shadow Dog Press and The SDL Review antholo-journal.

When she isn't creating, you can find her in her cottage garden with a cup of coffee and Leia, the elder cat, or out hiking with her dogs, Shadow and Padmé, in the Berkshires and beyond.

Learn more about C at CBMottor.com

900
E Union
At
Katy's
By Leland
Seese
20

Every dog is known by name,
knows the crumbs
across the floor are for the taking.

There will never be a Katy's II
or Katy's East. Katy keeps it local
at 20th and Union. Her business model

is "Just be miraculous." It's warm
in winter, cool in summer, capacious
though comprising three small tables.

Her secret is the light that shines
behind her bright brown eyes,
a genuine *It's great to know you, friend!*

Coffee, breakfast sandwiches, hugs,
and laughter to a soundtrack called
Whatever the Barista on This Shift

Might Need to Feel Today.
If you drive a Maserati, don't stride in
as if you own the place.

You can wait your turn behind the man
who spent the night curled in a doorway
cocooned in fentanyl.

Katy knows that guy by name,
never charges for a BLT and joe.
You be a regular like all the other dogs.

Martin was from Marshalltown
in Iowa,

onetime J. C. Penney clerk,
former fundamentalist.

His smile, incapable of guile
underneath his dorky mustache,

was kinder than the store's
automatic sliding doors

gliding open into air-
conditioned budget opulence,

sweltered August,
Midwestern afternoons.

When we met at seminary,
Martin's mind became

my personal *Pygmalion*.
You've never heard of Henry Rollins?

You've never seen Eraserhead?
I spun some vinyl — Hendrix

axe theatrics, Miles Davis'
modal jazz, *Madama Butterfly*.

Dragged him to a film series,
Akira Kurosawa's *Rashomon*,

The Seven Samurai.
At my church in Marshalltown

he shouted over "London Calling"
we burned books like yours,

Smashed records with a hammer.
Martin wasn't burning up

my bookshelves. My records
started going home with him.

Transformation came
the way a tickle in your throat

foretells a coming cold.
In a class on Kierkegaard

Martin raised his hand,
smiled his smile, asked

a question, brought the lecture
to a halt. *A seminary class called*

The Theology of Kierkegaard –
isn't that an oxymoron?

Our professor, flipping pages
frantically in Fear and Trembling,

gaped, stared out a window,
said, *Huh, yeah. I guess it is.*

End of our first year. Martin
took me on New Jersey Transit,

midnight to Manhattan, subway
to East Village, a club called 8BC.

He smiled, standing on the sidewalk.
That guy there is in the band tonight,

They Might Be Giants.
I'd like to introduce you.

By Leland Seese

east to princeton

Leland Seese

cicadas sizzle
in branches

of white ashes
full throttle

miniature maracas
bugs in heat

jersey drivers
buzz jug handles

fly around
the roundabouts

we're not in
seattle anymore

still newlyweds
we live for fun

full throttle in
our honda civic

weekends
down the shore

speeding toward
degree and graduation

marveling
at cardinals

fireflies
thunder's

dark
seduction

Leland Seese lives in Seattle, Washington. His poems appear in Frontier Poetry, The Chestnut Review, RHINO, The Stonecoast Review, and many other journals.

More of his poems can be found at

www.lelandseesepoetry.com.

From his website:

The poems gathered here comprise efforts to express a lifelong fascination with story and a hope of aligning formal theological training with a number of mystical experiences. I locate them in the events of my life as a member of families intact and dispersed, foster, adoptive, and biological; as an intrepid fan of baseball; and as one who catches glimpses of the numinous in all these things. My wife and I, and our six children, live in Seattle.

BORDER

Contemplate the effort to leave—the work
required: travel, save, love, hate

when necessary—dust
covered, money exchanged—fear

chasing across geography—only met
in separation

incarceration
decimation of dreams.

D. Larissa Peters

FIRST-BORN SON

D. LARISSA PETERS

It's his death day
they mark
because that's the day everything
changed for them.

And—for the rest of us —
daughters left behind.
An aftermath of
"personal Affects",
the untarnished memory,
odd feelings that
felt misplaced in a 5th grade classroom
— and the laughter
that felt misplaced
at home.

GERIATRIC HAPPINESS

D. LARISSA PETERS

It's hard to settle into this happiness -
—the tandem bike, looking at rings kind—

—the tiny kick, read all the books you can kind—

I've made sure, 100% sure that I was content,
happy. With the life can-be-an-adventure mentality, won't-let
anything-get-me-down kind

I won against the stereotype, the pressed down
patriarchy,
the religious family-style expectations.
I won so that
I didn't need them
And at 40, I was happy.

So this different kind, regular kind, this forever kind,
"I'm so happy for you" from others kind
feels strange, uncertain, surreal

Imposter

I'm still running as I leap off the cliff.

D Larissa Peters grew up in Indonesia and has been somewhat of a nomad. After meandering around the East Coast for more than 10 years, she now resides in California. Her most recently published poems have appeared in Eastern Iowa Review, Onyx Etched Magazine, and a few forthcoming pieces elsewhere.

More of her work can be found at
inotherwordspoetry.com.

Twitter: @LarissaPeters
Instagram: @mango_poetry

PHOTOSHOOT FANTASIES

SAM HENDRIAN

Rolled her eyes at Time's #1
Dressed to the nines for the 99th time,
Wishing they would move over
And let Jane Doe have a chance.

She thought if she could look beautiful for a day
She'd feel beautiful for a lifetime,
Finally cognizant
Of her full potential.

Also feared addiction
To fashionable fiction,
Becoming the very person
She rolled her eyes at.

It was bound to backfire either way
As old acquaintances came out of the woodworks
And told her she looked good
To affirm she didn't before.

So she kept on her jeans and Gene Kelly disposition
Dancing on over to the donut shop
Where she courted temporary pregnancy
Because no one was looking there anyway.

WORDLESS TRUTH

—SAM HENDRIAN

Hugged one second longer
Than our usual front seat farewells,
Subtly adding an extra squeeze
So you'd know how hard it was to leave.

Words are wasted far too much
By those overwhelmed with the wordless
And I was not about to risk
The truth sounding like a checklist.

Besides, you still weren't ready
For such a revelation
Even if it's already been revealed
In our little silent ways.

Of course, some say a sudden meteor
Ending everything
Might make us regret the phrase we regret
While waiting for the so-called proper time.

Well, we woke up another day
Which means there's more space to convey
The take-it-or-leave-it breakthrough
That I love you.

BLANKET

SAM HENDRIAN

We asked each other casually
If we'd recently met other people
While pretending the answers bore no impact
On the rest of our conversation.

It's become a tradition for me
To meet the perfect person at the wrong time
Like a museum patron gazing at a portrait
Painted 90 years ago.

She theorized herself into oblivion –
Maybe I'll do this, maybe I'll do that –
Whereas me myself was happy
With the love I already knew for sure.

Perhaps I wouldn't mind being a rock star spouse
Expecting frequent dalliances
But not particularly bothered
Because I'm the one they come home to.

Anyhow, we continued to discuss noteworthy encounters
Even though none of them compared
With the warm trustworthy blanket
Spread across our trembling legs.

SKIN AND BONES

SAM HENDRIAN

Snuck into the back of the classroom
To learn about intimacy,
The rotating voices of substitute teachers
Barely registering where I sat.

Received simple instructions
On how to turn a face into a symbol,
A symbol into pleasure,
Pleasure into satisfaction.

The last part was optional of course
Since throughout all of human history
The only ones who've died satisfied
Are the voluntarily uneducated.

We were warned that someday skin
Would cease to cause excitement
And we'd be stuck fantasizing
About the bones beneath.
I fell asleep midway through the lecture
Then dreamed of a face-to-face conversation
Which radiated symbolic pleasure
Plus a fragment of satisfaction.

SHOWED PROMISE

SAM HENDRIAN

Stumbled across the obituary at precisely 12:00,
The usual time for mid-year New Year's resolutions
As the drunkenness turns to queasiness
And the pleasure starts to sting.

26 and two days counting;
Didn't even have the glory of 27,
Just a halfway thought-out header
That read, "Showed Promise."

Showed promise for what exactly?
Capitalistic success?
Perhaps a Wikipedia page
Or picture on a restaurant wall?

Anyhow, it didn't matter;
Whatever promise was shown had faded
Unless there was an accompanying suicide note
To inspire posthumous adulation.

Wandered to the cemetery the next morning,
Paid respects from a stranger
Which are sometimes sincerer
Than the rehearsed well-wishes of a friend.

Assured him he was more
Than what he had not yet become
And that what he already was
Was all he ever needed to be.

Sam Hendrian is a lifelong storyteller striving to foster empathy through art. He resides in Los Angeles, where he primarily works as a poet/independent filmmaker and makes at least one movie per month. You can find links to his art on Instagram.

instagram.com/samhendrian143

I WAS RIGHT

LAURA SHELL

He died.

Something I fed him ruptured his gut, and that's all I'm going to say about that.

I took him to the emergency vet because his stomach was distended, and he was breathing heavily, which meant he was in pain. Due to the x-rays, the vet wanted to keep him overnight. I agreed, believing I would pick him up the next morning and he would be cured.

But no.

I got a call from the vet stating that he had "gone downhill overnight," and the technicians were doing CPR on him as I was talking to the vet on the phone. The vet wanted to put him down, and I told him, "You do all you can to keep him alive!"

"Looks like he's trying to go on his own anyway."

After that devastating call, I got dressed to go to the vet, and I phoned my friend, Terry, screaming, "he's dying."

After a 52-minute drive to the vet, I was taken into a room and graciously told that Groot did not make it. The pain in my chest had me kicking the nearest table and spewing a slew of curses. The room blurred through my tears.

The vet came in and said words, but I couldn't comprehend the sounds emanating from his mouth. My dog was dead.

MY DOG WAS DEAD!

They gave me his body in a nice canvas bag, which I placed on the passenger seat of my car.

I was so hysterical that I barely remembered the 52-minute drive home—except when I was pulled over for passing vehicles over the double yellow line.

Really?

The officer saw how upset I was and noticed my dog's body on the passenger seat; he gave me a warning instead of a ticket and said some words like that vet had, which I don't remember either.

I also don't remember driving the rest of the way home.

I left his body in the car until my husband came home.

I watched him dig the hole in the yard while I held Groot in my arms. Then, I gingerly placed him in the hole.

My husband made me place a shovel of soil on top of him.

And I lost it.

I wailed and screamed and wailed again. I couldn't see anything through my tears. My knees buckled, and I fell to the ground. My husband (who never cries) had to pick me up. My feet dragged along the earth as we headed toward the patio. He placed me in a chair.

I wondered if he could smell the booze on my breath.

Yes, I had broken five years of sobriety and had four shots of bourbon before he got home.
But I felt justified in doing so.

Once I calmed down a little, I looked at my husband straight in the eyes, although my view
was askew from the alcohol and tears, and said, "We have to get another dog."

It was the only thing I knew of that would take the edge off, hinder, or flat-out get rid of the
unholy pain of losing a pet.

I was right.

Ten days later, we got a female dog named Grits.

Sure, the primary purpose of getting her was to lessen the pain of losing Groot. But she's her
own little entity—an angel and a devil. She loves to give kisses and shit on the floor.
Everything is a toy to her, not just her dog toys, but shoes and toilet paper.

So, giving our attention to this six-pound animal has left little room for anything else, which
includes mourning Groot.

I was right.

Laura Shell has been published in NUNUM, Maudlin House, Typishly, The Citron Review, and many others. Her first anthology of paranormal stories, The Canine Collection, was released in 2024. She's a prolific writer and submitter of flash fiction and the Editor of the Flash Phantoms horror fiction site–www.flashphantoms.net.

You can find more about her at
laurashellhorror.wordpress.com.

CONNECTIONS

SCOTT ORTOLANO

In the land of Jaödeogë, at the point where the Allegheny, Monongahela and Ohio Rivers wend together, lies the outline of Fort Pitt, its remains eclipsed by towering skyscrapers and palatial sports stadiums. In quiet moments, Luke can just remember, sitting in the park's center and slowly tracing a finger along the concrete outline of this lost world. Its cold firmness strangely at odds with the soft tufts of carefully manicured grass. Caressing the earth, he focuses, trying to rebuild the walls in his mind, tightly shutting his eyes against the slurred shouts of his parents, longing to slip through the fort's spiraling skeleton… into the past… or, simply, nothingness.

The Pittsburgh river walk is decorated with seasonal flowers and monuments to the people responsible for what the city has become. Just as numerous are the encampments, blooming with the many-colored tents of those that society has forgotten, flowers accented by broken and missing teeth, crumpled cans of Keystone Light, empty syringes, and fragment-filled garbage bags. The camps endure through the clearances of embarrassed politicians, perhaps shifting locations but always springing back to life, self-seeding urban flora belonging just as much to the city as the celebrated wildflowers that bloom atop the West End Overlook each spring. The tents, like the foundations of the fort, and the lost graves of the Monongahela, stand as silent reminders of what has been sacrificed for the harvests of progress.

Sitting on the porch, Luke softly exhales cigarette smoke against the crumbling wall of his aunt's Florida duplex—he and his sister's final retreat from a father consumed with nodding off into dreamscapes of pure white bliss and a mother forever trapped within the hazes of alcohol-induced stupors. The last message from his father was a dinosaur birthday card, the number ten standing out in shiny reflective letters on the unsigned surface. Buried in his dresser drawer, the T-Rex's eyes still roll, forever moorless in their plastic prisons.

Luke takes another drag and moves his hand lightly over the flowing wall, following the blue stucco's twisting pattern. His thoughts drift again back to the slow rivers of childhood, to the Three Sisters bridges, suspended yellow-beam monoliths of steel, concrete, and cable, inextricably tying disparate shores into a single divided home. On one of his last days at the park, he had looked up to see a man jump from the Roberto Clemente Bridge. The legged dot moved slowly at first, suspended in midair, arms flailing, before quickly accelerating down into the gloom below. What he wouldn't give to have been so consumed, to be embraced in the tight loving arms of those dark waters.

Scott Ortolano is an English professor at Florida SouthWestern State College. His poetry and prose have recently appeared in Ponder Review, Across The Margin, Hawai`i Pacific Review, Rathalla Review, Blood+Honey, and Apocalypse Confidential. You can usually find him reading, wandering, fishing, or frantically grading—often with his two children in tow. Follow him on Bluesky at @floridasnow.bsky.social and Instagram at florida_snow_. More of his work is available at www.SOrtolano.com

EXECUTIVE ORDER PROTECTING THE AMERICAN PEOPLE AGAINST INVASION, SECTION 9

BY
FELICITY LANDA

There's an infinity between
chocolate fingerprints on drywall
and what continues to be forever
lost to the trees— construct of
what is seen as geometry
wall slides into wall with pocket secrets
they call doors and windows

there is no home other than this place
where they chatter, bare feet
in bath water, believers leaving traces
in liquid wax of glass fathers
          Santa Maria prega
          para nosotros
light one for me, when I leave

cleaving what they sewed into tapestry
for the mother she was meant to be —
American dream— he sang — unfinished
beat by beat. Build it behind our feet
carve the puzzle piece from strawberry field
to the home on the hill the very tile beneath
which the blood from the saw cut on my hand
will breathe what is then and can only be
my documented infinity.

WHEN SERINA COMES TO TOWN

BY FELICITY LANDA

My father bought us a bag of pan dulce when my cousin came to stay the night, cut them into pieces on a tray so we could taste every kind. The moment is captured in a photo of our crooked tooth smiles, limbs pinned to our sides, scrunched eyes, heads tilted and bodies melting into the counter-top. We dipped into the fragrant clouds, dissolving magic in our mouths, crackling sugar surrendered to sand in our hands and I thought this is what sin tastes like, an unholy treason to my mother's persistence on royal jelly with whole wheat toast, torturing the soul, clogging the throat. When I see conchas now I remember how we used to believe in beautiful things like sugar on our lips, misty dough kisses, drips of honey forever lovely on our fingertips. And I miss my dad and how ecstatic I was to see that bag of treats, that I don't think he actually bought we just forgot it was my Aunt who brought them as an offering to our coven of cousin love, not-so-little-anymore girl laughter, secrets pop rock explosions rolling off the tongue, golden woven to hold us closer until the morning. But still I think only of the way he cut the pan dulce on that tray, my father, who was colder than most, sarcastic and quick to admonish, always tired because he could never sleep deeply, the way he should have been able to, the way we would later, hair and legs tangled in a maze of argyle blankets, bellies full of the sweetest kind of safety.

BABY TEETH

FELICITY LANDA

I collect baby teeth
in the corner of my jewelry box
cavernous bloody baby teeth
like pearls, like fish scales
like mirrored half moons

broken shells edged
to the rhythm of constellations.
There is enough to love
in ordinary things— baby teeth
or rivered fingerprints on
television screens

found only when breaking
ground on new soil, reminders
of what it was like before
teeth— when fresh unaltered flesh
forgives and gives so easily.

It's there where I'll grow old
bones never rot they just erode
like rocks into sand, like ocean
over land, like you and me into
baby feet, hands, eyes, ears, and nose
they two— the sacred, the bones

dropping teeth for me to hold
filling me with the shed
of wild dead things, after taking
what I've grown. I give it all
for this fragment of her smile

now piled in the corner of my
jewelry box, where I'll hide
this singular truth— a tooth
blunt enough to break us loose:

there is no going back to before
when I loved like a fresh stretch
of jagged shore before a storm.
I collect baby teeth because
I've forgotten how to let go.

MY DAUGHTERS ARE PLAYING ORPHANS AGAIN

FELICITY LANDA

The three-year-old said pretend our dad died
and what they don't know is their father
isn't here because he's in Arizona
what they don't know is that trip to
Scottsdale in the middle of August is in
desperation of the correct diagnosis
what they don't know is what we've
always believed to be his joints we now know
may be his heart what they don't know
is how easy it is for an organ to stop
how rare it is to take a breath
how many valves and paths must connect
what they don't know is how soft a body is
beneath its bones how delicate a chest
how precious for two souls to find each other
within the mess, what they won't know
until they grow older is how his heart pumps
blood to the same hands that make the nerves
in the side of my neck pulse when we touch
constricting my throat when I think about
how those hands would feel cold— lifeless
is not quite death and yet we drift there
wait for relief or tragedy wait breathe and
dream, play pretend like we don't understand
exactly what it means to die.

WATCHING BLUEY
ON A SATURDAY NIGHT

FELICITY LANDA

I remember when Sarah laughed for the first time
in the baby carrier, sunlight through closed blinds
bottom floor of the 500 square foot home
where we spent the first year of her life.

The moment is memorable only by
the iPhone video that captured the hiccup hitch
laughter, pre-disaster, a baby strapped to your chest
light— like the flutter of butterfly wings and you seemed

new. I dissect the memory of you
because of the way time tastes bitter
but deeply familiar. I measure the years
by what you are capable of carrying without pain

the reasons I've found to blame everyone else
but myself, for the words I say when I feel
like the substance of a lifetime lied
about its weight.

I love you— I understand now what that means
because Sarah has grown, and I still hold her
wait for her laughter, then look to you to make sure
you heard it too.

Felicity Landa is a Chicana writer with an MFA from UC Riverside Palm Desert. Her work has appeared in Pithead Chapel, The Sunlight Press, Capulet Mag, Lit Angels and elsewhere. She is a current Periplus Fellow and was a 2022 Mentee for the Latinx in Publishing mentorship program. She lives with her family in Santa Barbara, California. You can read more of her work at felicitylanda.com

ABSENCE

QUINN DEWEY

I have been told that absence makes the heart
Grow fonder, but I have been gone longer
Than I would have liked, and I don't know if
My feelings for you can get much stronger.

What's six months have compared to eight years?
Depends. How many stolen kisses shared
While dancing in the kitchen get missed as
Time drips through glass, fine as salt in the air?

I don't want to hear how fast the time goes.
Tell me you love me, as if I don't know.

Quinn Dewey is an author based in the Pacific North West. He lives with his lovely wife and powerful daughter. His nonfiction work has been published in the Washburn Review, he has a short story published in the anthology series "Dead Girls Walking: The Green Volume," and poetry published in WIREWORM Magazine. He is a supporting member of the Horror Writers Association.

SUPERPOWER
By
Thomas Behan
EXIT

I stare through the back of all their heads
from the last row of a packed flight.
There are no faces to obfuscate the truth,
just mine. Peering MRI-like, I come to
know. Know now that they are afraid.

Of being found out. Of not being prepared.
Of versions of the future without them in it.
Of staying a secret from everyone forever.
Of the possibility they are living in a simulation.

That they are going to lose control of their bowels
someday in a room full of people. Maybe on
a flight, when the Fasten Seatbelts sign is on and
the unempathetic flight attendant prioritizes
their idea of the big picture.

That their mother lied, and their father was right.
That they are broken in a unique way that will
never happen again on Earth and that is the only
thing that will ever be special about them.

That this is the least amount of scaly skin they
will ever have. That somewhere their misdeeds are
being tracked and summed rather than averaged.
That the thing that will kill them has been
active for years, hiding in plain sight
because they don't know where to look.

That life is just a movie, and
they are hardly in any of it.

Functional
FUNERAL

THOMAS BEHAN

I think people die so The People can cry.
To purge the toxins of accumulated sadness
within the acceptable bounds of the social contract.

Already nature has reclaimed and
repurposed her to fertilize tears.
The solid sheet of plate glass indifference
that stood the test of time suddenly breaks
with the ease of tissue paper.

This one, the bawler who
decided every day not to connect.
That one, the other bawler, incapable
of having a lower priority than
visiting the diminishing mother in life.

Maler mounds red, wet and bloated.
No training necessary, it just happens.
Like all of nature's best ideas.

The new corpse of the old lady,
who wondered about her
low place in the pecking order,
finally has no opinion on the matter.

Her inaction is the action.
A highlight reel tells a story
no one remembers so The People
don't have to talk amongst
themselves excessively.

Thank you, Grandma, for sadness.
Your last gift, your best gift.
At last, something we can use.

Thomas is a writer from Northern Virginia USA and his work has been published in many literary journals including Isele Magazine, Cinnabar Moth Literary Collections, The Brussels Review, as well as The George Washington University Press. His literary fiction short story "Symbiosis" was published in Secant Publishing's anthology "Best Stories on the Human Impact of Climate Change" and that story is nominated for the Secant Publishing Prize. His collection of short stories, "Life in the Demilitarized Zone," has been published by Alien Buddha Press. Thomas was in the running as a finalist in last year's Tennessee Williams and New Orleans Literary Festival.

ABOUT SHADOW DOG PRESS

What We Publish

At Shadow Dog Press, we publish little books that make a big impact, including gorgeous chapbooks, collections, and novellas. We are also home to The SDL Review, a quarterly antholo-journal and our founder's labor of love.

Our Publishing Model

We follow a traditional publishing model with competitive royalties, transparent contracts, and varied advances. We do not require signed authors to pay for services or share in costs, and we never require them to make any kind of purchase.

Our Acquisitions Process

Shadow Dog Press acquires most titles through contests and open submission periods and does not accept unsolicited manuscripts outside of these methods.

"We are drawn to evocative, raw, poignant, and powerful pieces of substance and style. Pluck at our heartstrings, speak to our souls, send shivers down our spines, shine a light on our darkness, and uncover our unspoken truths."

More About Shadow Dog Press

We are a small independent press started in 2024 and located in North Adams, Massachusetts, a tiny Appalachian Trail town in the Northern Berkshires.

Shadow Dog Press was founded on the profound belief that poets and writers hold the power to transcend boundaries, foster empathy, enhance understanding, and catalyze social change. We envision a world where poetry serves as a bridge between differing human experiences, and where stories from all corners of society are not only heard but celebrated. Literature, we believe, should reflect the complexity of human life, acting as a catalyst for dialogue and societal transformation. We aim to challenge the homogeneity often found in mainstream literary circles by offering a broader, more accurate view of the human condition.

We are advocates of a literary renaissance. Through our work, we hope to inspire a new generation of poets, writers, and readers who see themselves in the pages of the books they encounter, and in doing so, contribute to a more accurate literary legacy.

The Shadow Dog Vision for the Future

Commitment to Poets

We aim to enrich the literary landscape by actively seeking out, acquiring, publishing, and promoting profound works of poetry with our focus dedicated to amplifying the voices of poets exhibiting excellence in their craft regardless of background or education, providing them with publishing opportunities, and, as we grow- awards, grants and scholarships that acknowledge their contributions and encourage their continued creativity. Shadow Dog Press recognizes that accurate representation in literature goes beyond token gestures. We are committed to:

Publishing Excellence:

We will maintain high editorial standards for our acquisitions while ensuring that the selection process prioritizes excellence in literature and honors the nuances of their narratives. We invest the funds right back into the Shadow Dog Literary nonprofit mission.

Financial Support:

Through fair contracts, grants, scholarships, and awards, we aim to alleviate some of the financial burdens that can hinder poets, allowing them the space and resources to write without the constant pressure of economic constraints.

Career Development:

Through The SDL Review, we aim to offer a vital platform for emerging poets and writers from outside the academic realm by providing opportunities to develop their craft and establish their reputation while they prepare for full-length publication. We're currently working to develop mentorship, workshops, and professional development opportunities to help authors navigate the literary world, from manuscript preparation to promotion and beyond.

Public Engagement, Educational Outreach, and Literacy Initiatives for 2026 and Beyond

Our commitment extends into the community with a focus on education and public engagement:

Literary Events

Shadow Dog Press plans to host a variety of events, including readings, book launches, panel discussions, book fairs, conventions, and open mics that celebrate the works of American poets and writers. These events will engage avid readers and those new to literary arts alike.

Educational Outreach

Programs aimed at schools, libraries, and community centers to promote literacy, with a special emphasis on the importance of literature in understanding our society. The SDL Review will also highlight newly released works by writers and poets with editorial reviews and analysis, while also engaging readers by making the Review an interactive space where they can actively participate in the literary conversation by submitting their own reviews, opinions, and analytical articles.

At Shadow Dog, we are advocates for a literary renaissance. We believe in the power of poetry to change minds, hearts, and societies. Our ongoing efforts will be to ensure that literature is a true reflection of humanity, driving us toward a more empathetic, informed, and just world. Through our work, we hope to inspire a new generation of poets, writers, and readers who see themselves in the pages of the books they encounter, and in doing so, contribute to a more accurate literary legacy.

The SDL Review Contributor's Fund

Help us stay true to our commitment to publish and reward literary excellence by paying writers & poets for their contributions to The SDL Review.

HELP US GROW

All donations to The Contributor's fund go to paying and elevating writers, as well as transaction, platform, and administrative fees associated with doing so. Shadow Dog Press & The SDL Review were started with seed money scraped together by working-class writers. We're run by volunteers and have no large sponsors at this time, so every little bit helps.

Scan the QR code to learn more.

FALL 2025

IS BROUGHT TO YOU BY

. . .

C.B.Mottor
MEDIA

JM
CARPENTRY

SPECIAL THANKS

Dan in the Sun
James Mullen
Journey Bleu
Stu Bronstein
Leigh Sewell
James McLeish
Brandon James
Steve Malley
Jim Feenstra
Jonathan Wade
Jim Mentink
Spirits of Idaho

FROM THE SPRING 2025 ISSUE

- HAPPY HERE
- MY FATHER'S CLOSET
- THE FENCE
- THE DECISION AND THE DOG
- THANKS FOR THE EVIDENCE
- THE NECKLACE
- DRYWALL PIECES
- PRETTY POISON
- DIONYSUS

FROM THE SUMMER 2025 ISSUE

- AT KATY'S
- MARTIN
- EAST TO PRINCETON
- BORDER
- FIRST-BORN SON
- GERIATRIC HAPPINESS
- PHOTOSHOOT FANTASIES
- WORDLESS TRUTH
- BLANKET
- SKIN AND BONES
- SHOWED PROMISE
- I WAS RIGHT

FROM THE FALL 2025 ISSUE

- CONNECTIONS
- EXECUTIVE ORDER PROTECTING THE AMERICAN PEOPLE FROM INVASION, SECTION 9
- WHEN SERENA COMES TO TOWN
- BABY TEETH
- MY DAUGHTERS ARE PLAYING ORPHANS AGAIN
- WATCHING BLUEY ON A SATURDAY NIGHT
- ABSENCE
- SUPERPOWER
- FUNCTIONAL FUNERAL

Shadow Dog
PRESS

www.ingramcontent.com/pod-product-compliance
Lightning Source LLC
Chambersburg PA
CBHW020936310726
48980CB00007B/800/J

* 9 7 9 8 9 9 3 5 6 8 2 1 8 *